To_____

From_____

PILGRIMS QUOTATION SERIES
General Editor: Chaitanya Nagar

Life

Published by:
PILGRIMS PUBLISHING

An imprint of:
PILGRIMS BOOK HOUSE
B 27/98 A-8, Nawabganj Road
Durga Kund
Varanasi, India 221010
Telephone: 91-542-314060, 312496
Fax: 91-542-314059
E-mail: pilgrims@satyam.net.in
Website: www.pilgrimsbooks.com

Art Director: Dr. Sasya
Contributing Editor: John Snyder
Contributing Text Researchers: Dominic Di Zinno
and Chaitanya Nagar
Typeset by Naresh Subba and Biju John

Cover Photo by Deepankar Aron

1st Edition
Copyright © 2000, Pilgrims Publishing

ISBN 81-7769-037-X

Printed in India

Life

PILGRIMS

PILGRIMS PUBLISHING

Varanasi ◆ Kathmandu

All you need in this life is
ignorance and confidence;
and success is sure.

— MARK TWAIN
When Huck Finn Went to Highbrow

Three passions, simple but overwhelmingly strong, have governed my life: the longing for love, the search for truth, and unbearable pity for the suffering of mankind.

—BERTRAND RUSSELL
Autobiography

If 'A' is success in life, then A = x + y + z. Work is 'x', play is 'y', and 'z' is keeping your mouth shut.

—ALBERT EINSTEIN
In the 'Observer', 15 June 1950

I feel that life is...is divided
up into the horrible
and the miserable.

— ANONYMOUS.

The man that feels there is
no meaning in not only his
life, but in the lives of all
creatures, is not only
unhappy, but hardly fit for
living.

— ALBERT EINSTEIN
Ideas and Opinions

We make war that
we may live in peace.

—ARISTOTLE
Nicomachean Ethics

Living is my job
and my art.

—MONTAIGNE
Essais Essais

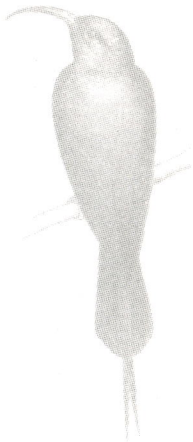

Life is one long process
of getting tired.

—SAMUEL BUTLER
Notebooks

Anyone can
stop a man's life,
but no one his death.

—SENECA
Phoenissae

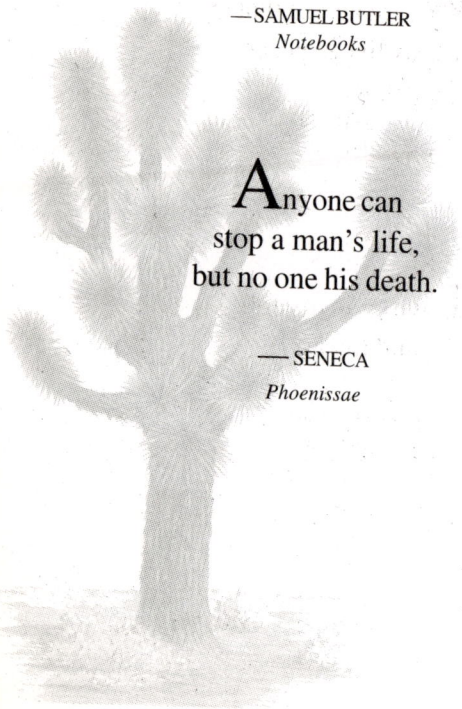

Life exists in the universe
only because a carbon atom
possesses certain exceptional
qualities.

—THE MYSTERIOUS UNIVERSE

Life is a foreign language;
all men mispronounce it.

—CHRISTOPHER MORLEY
Thunder on the Left

Life is a gamble at
terrible odds. If it were a bet,
you wouldn't take it.

— TOM STOPPARD
Rosencrantz and Guildenstern are Dead

Life is a horizontal fall.

— JEAN COCTEAU
Opium

Life is just one damned
thing after another.

—ELBERT HUBBARD
Philistine

Life is too short to
stuff a mushroom.

—SHIRLEY CONRAN
Superwoman

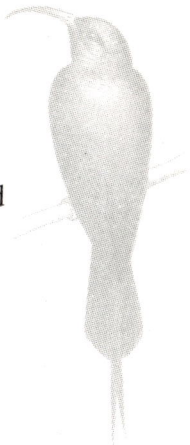

The intellect of man is
forced to choose perfection
of the life, or of the work.

— W. B. YEATS
Coole Park and Ballyee

To fear love is to fear life,
and those who fear life are
already three parts dead.

— BERTRAND RUSSELL
Marriage and Morals

The life of every man
is a diary in which
he means to
write one story,
and writes another;
and his humblest hour
is when he compares
the volume as it is with
what he vowed to make it.

— SIR J M BARRIE
The Little Minister

There is love of course.
And then there is life,
it's enemy.

—ANONYMOUS

Did you know that 'if' is
the middle word in life?

—DENNIS HOPPER
Apocalypse Now

Life is too short for chess.

—H J BYRON
Our Boys

There is no wealth but life.

—JOHN RUSKIN
Time and Tide

The value of life lies not in the length of days, but in the use you make of them...Whether you have lived enough depends not on the number of years but on your will.

—MONTAIGNE
Essais Essais

The unexamined life
is not worth living.

— ATTRIBUTED TO SOCRATES BY
PLATO
The Republic

Life, believe,
is not a dream,
so dark as sages say;
oft a little morning rain
foretells a pleasant day!

—CHARLOTTE BRONTE

Life consists in what
man is thinking of all day.

—EMERSON
Journals

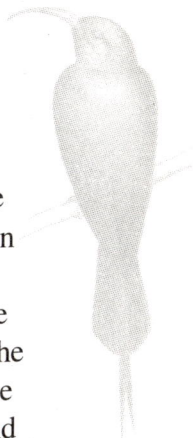

I am convinced that the world is not a mere bog in which men and women trample themselves in the mire and die. Something the magnificent is taking place here amid the cruelties and tragedies, and the supreme challenge to intelligence is that of making the noblest and best in our curious heritage prevail.

— C A BEARD

Life's a long headache
in a noisy street.

—JOHN MASEFIELD
The Widow In The Bye Street

A living thing is
distinguished from a dead
thing by the multiplicity of the
changes at any moment taking
place in it.

—HERBERT SPENCER
Principles Of Biology

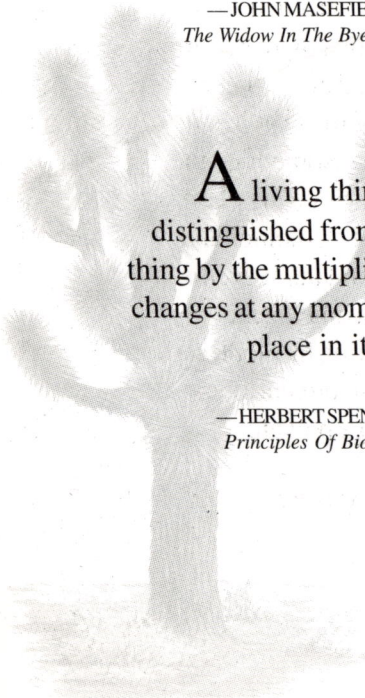

Life is but thought.

—S T COLERIDGE
Youth And Age

Life is a jest, and all
things show it:
I thought so once, but now
I know it.

—JOHN GAY
My Own Epitaph

All life is an experiment.
The more experiments you
make, the better.

—EMERSON
Journals

Life is a preparation for the
future; and the best
preparation for the future is
to live as if there were none.

—ELBERT HUBBARD
The Philistine

Life is a flame that is
always burning itself out,
but it catches fire again
every time a child is born.

— BERNARD SHAW
*The Adventures Of The Black Girl In Her
Search For God*

Life is a school of
probability.

—BAGEHOT
Literary Studies

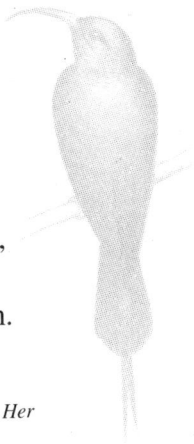

To live is like to love—
all reason is against it,
and all healthy instinct for it.

—SAMUEL BUTLER THE YOUNGER
Notebooks

Life is made up of
interruptions.

—W S GILBERT
Patience

Life is not a spectacle or a feast; it is a predicament.

— GEORGE SANTAYANA
Articles And Essays

Life is a boundless privilege, and when you pay for your ticket, and get into the car, you have no guess what good company you will find there.

— EMERSON
Conduct Of Life: Considerations By The Way

Life is like a library
owned by an author.
In it are a few books
which he wrote himself,
but most of them
were written for him.

—HARRY EMERSON FOSDICK
Sermon: Life

Our life consisteth partly
in folly, and partly in
wisdom.

—MONTAIGNE
Essays

Life is a smoke that curls—
   Curls in a flickering skein,
   That winds and whisks
         and whirls,
   A figment thin and vain,
   Into the vast inane.

—W E HENLEY
Of the Nothingness of Things

The less of routine,
   the more of life.

—A B ALCOTT
Table Talk: Habits

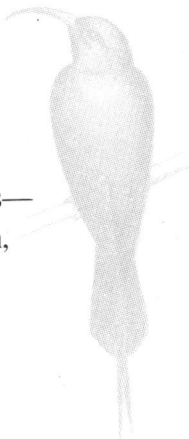

Life, like poverty,
makes strange bedfellows.

—BULWER-LYTTON
The Caxtons

Life is an end in itself,
and the only question as
to whether it is worth
living is whether you
have had enough of it.

—JUSTICE O W HOLMES

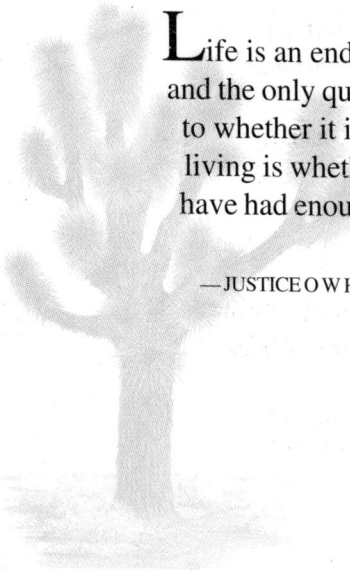

Is life worth living?
That depends on the liver!

—UNKNOWN
Is Life Worth Living?

Yes, my love,
whosoever lives,
loses . . . but he also wins.

—GOETHE
Stella

It gives proof of a great
heart to return to life
for the sake of others,
and noble men have
often done this.

— SENECA
Epistulae Ad Lucilium

My life is a battle.

— VOLTAIRE

Life is mostly froth
and bubble; two things
stand like stone:
Kindness in another's troubl
courage in your own.

— A L GORDON
Ye Weary Wayfarer

If life an empty bubble be,
how sad for those who cannot
see the rainbow in the
bubble!

— FLOCKER-LAMPSON
Bramble-Rise

Life and love
are all a dream.

— BURNS
Lament

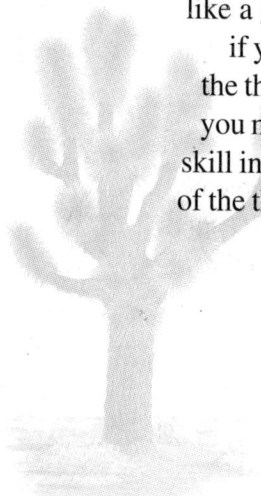

The life of man is
like a game with dice:
if you don't get
the throw you want,
you must show your
skill in making the best
of the throw you do get.

—TERENCE
Adelphi

Away with funeral music—
set the pipe to powerful lips—
the cup of life's for him
that drinks and not for him
that sips.

—R L STEVENSON
The Cup Of Life

This world is but a
thoroughfare full of woe,
And we but pilgrims passing
to and fro. Death is an end of
every worldly sore.

—CHAUCER
The Knight's Tale

I depart from life as from an inn, and not as from my home.

—CICERO
De Senectute

One life—a little gleam of Time between two eternities.

—CARLYLE
Heroes And Hero-worship

Life is a fortress which neither you nor I know anything about.

—NAPOLEON

We live amid surfaces, and the true art of life is to skate well on them.

—EMERSON
Essays, Second Series: Experience

You cannot learn to skate
without being ridiculous...
The ice of life is slippery.

— BERNARD SHAW
Fanny's First Play: Introduction

We live,
not as we wish,
but as we can.

—MENANDER
Andria

To be vulnerable is to live.
To withdraw is to die.

—J KRISHNAMURTI

Only a life lived for
others is a life worthwhile.

—ALBERT EINSTEIN

Brief and powerless is man's life; on him and all his race the slow, sure doom falls pitiless and dark.

—BERTAND RUSSELL

One's real life is so often the life that one does not lead.

—OSCAR WILDE

A tale told by an idiot—
full of sound and fury,
signifying nothing.

—SHAKESPEARE